TWEETS & FARTS
THE
FARTING BIRDS
COLORING BOOK

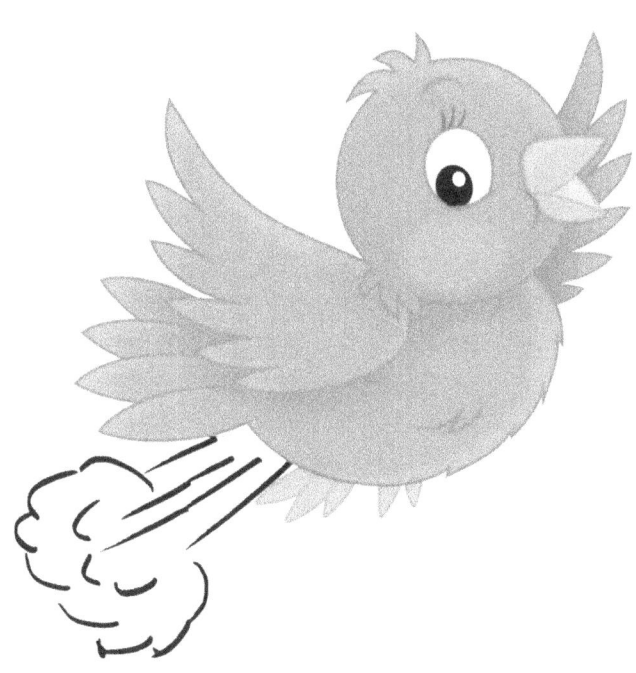

RAND M. VEKTOR

TWEETS & FARTS: THE FARTING BIRDS COLORING BOOK

Copyright © 2018 by Rand M. Vektor

All rights reserved. No part of this publication may be reproduced, distributed, or transmitted in any form or by any means, including photocopying, recording, or other electronic or mechanical methods.

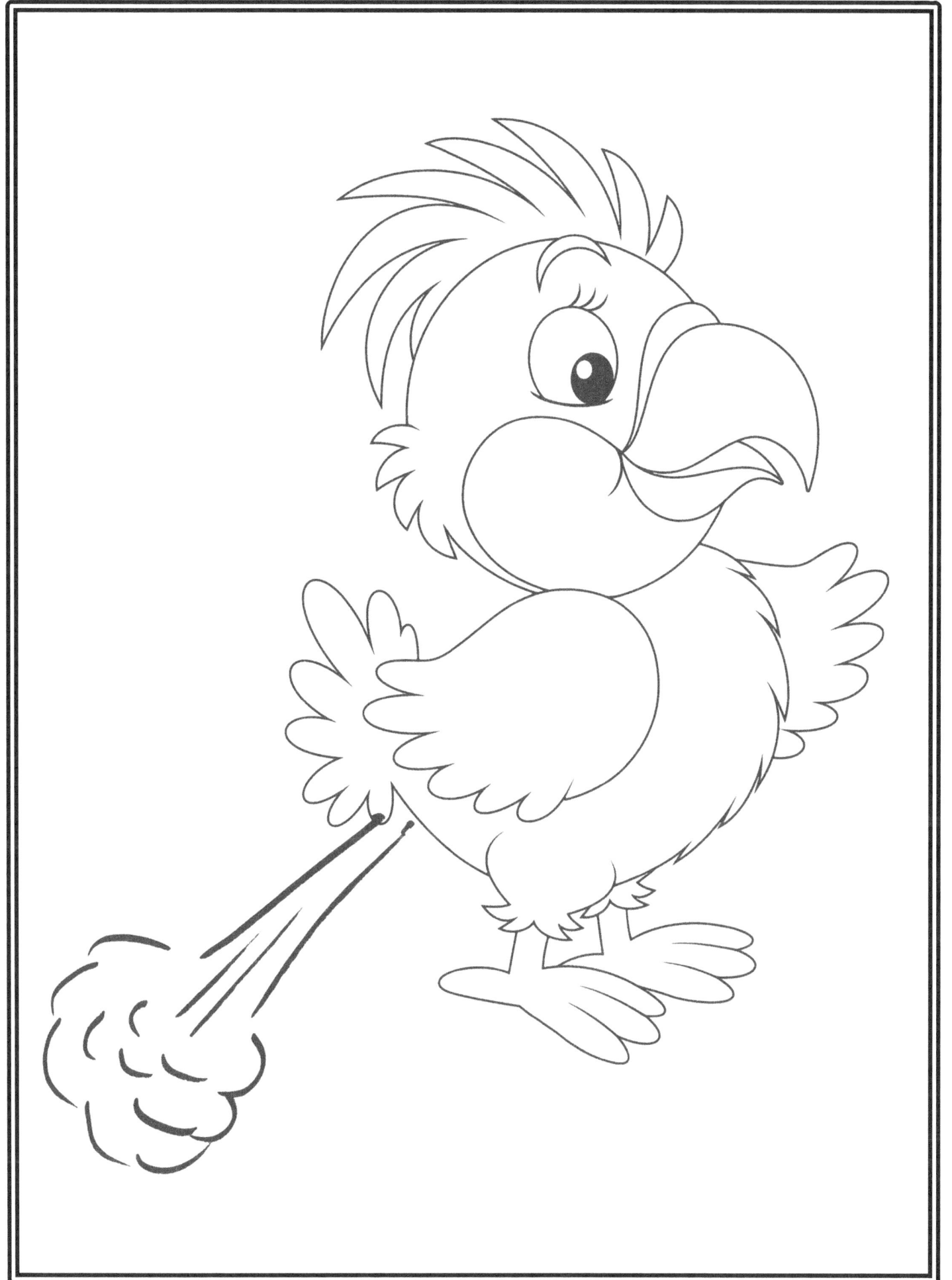

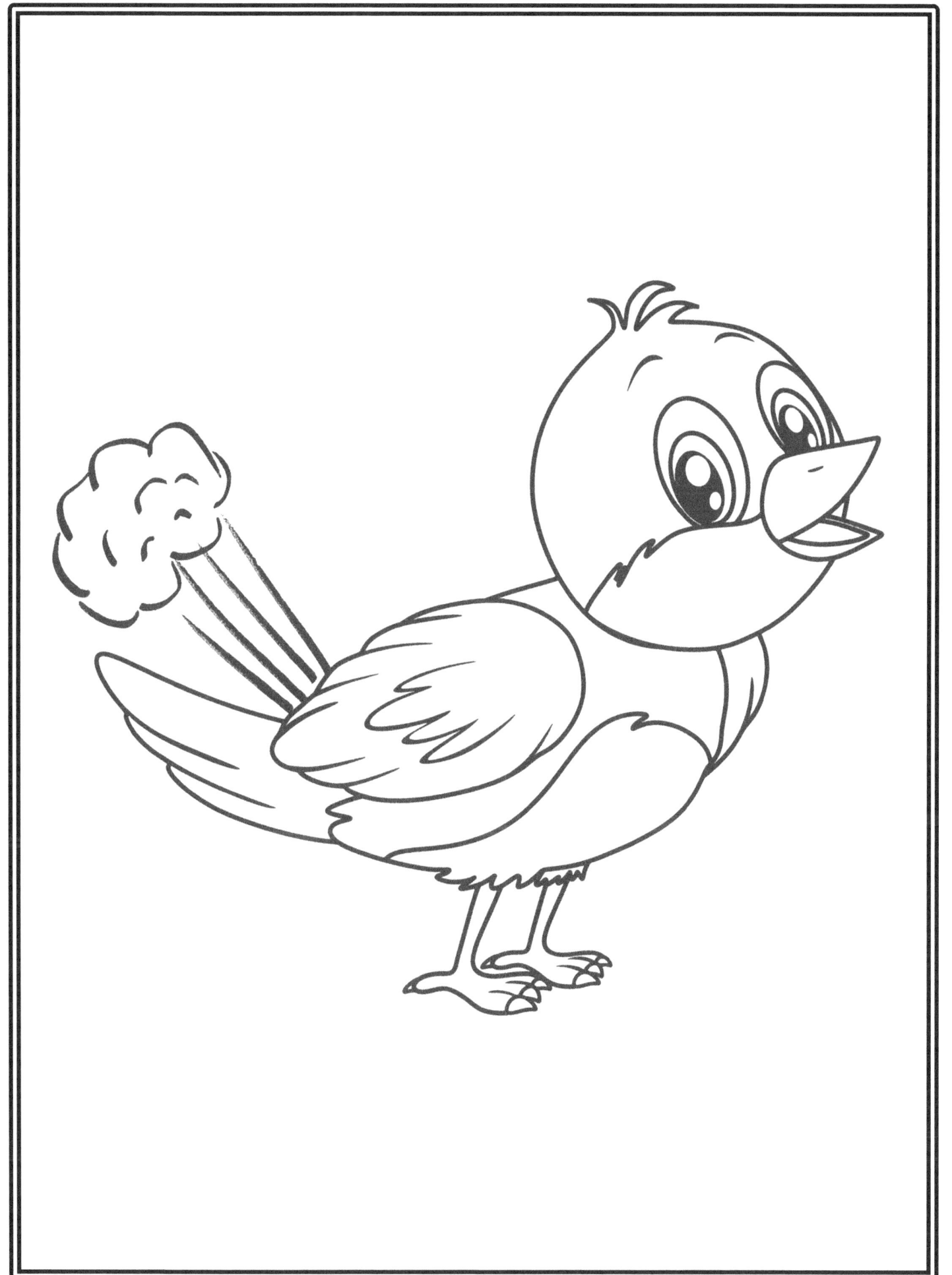

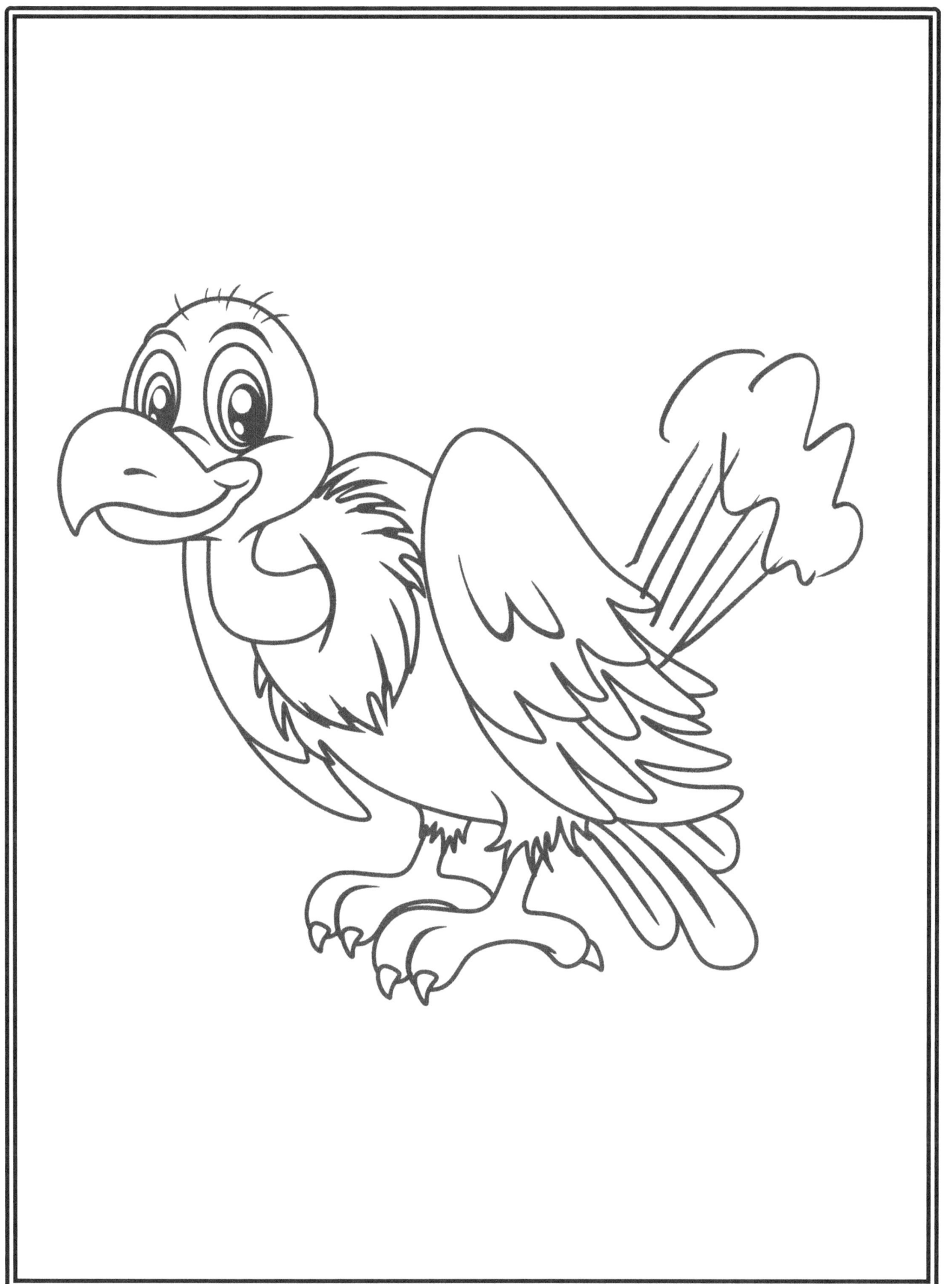

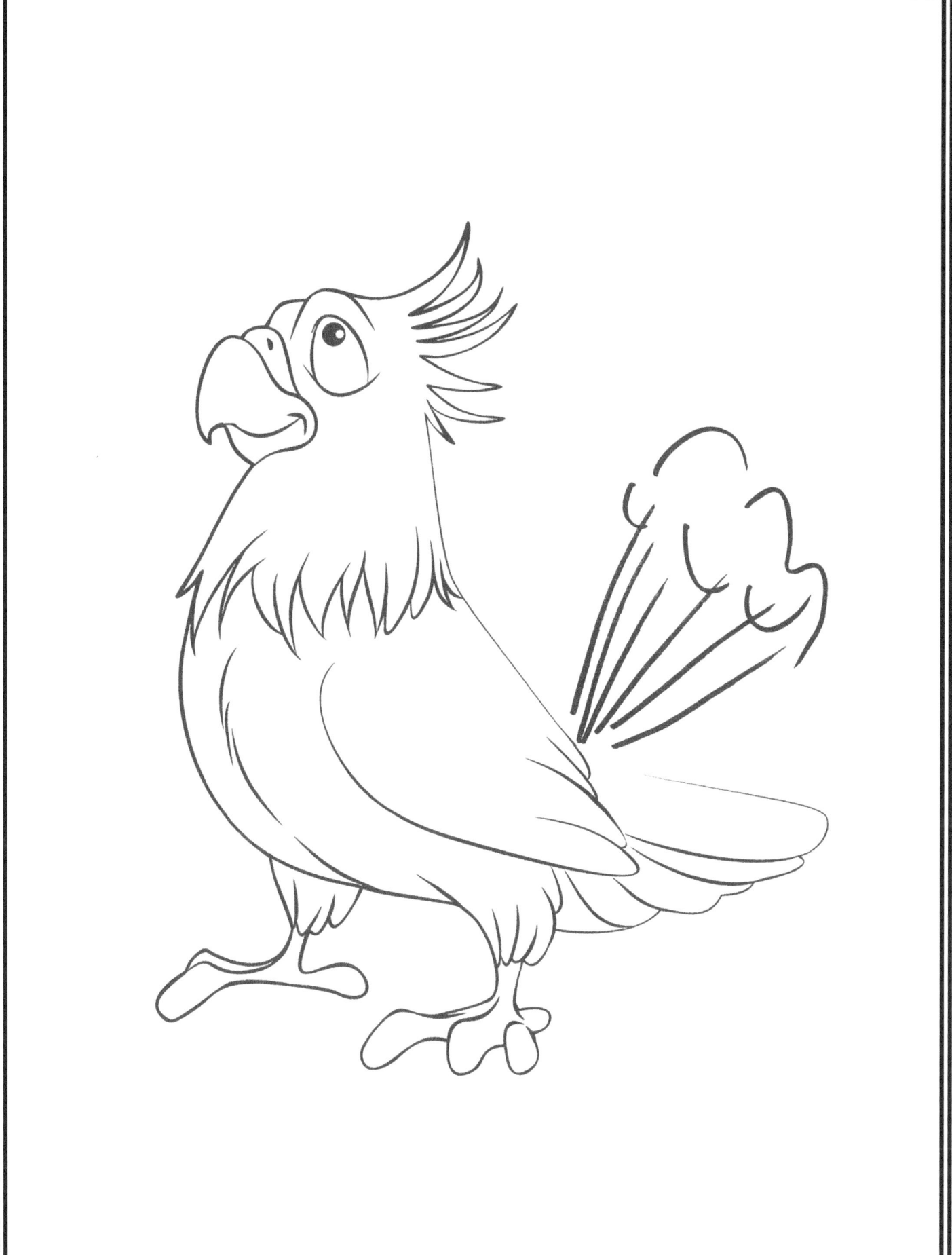

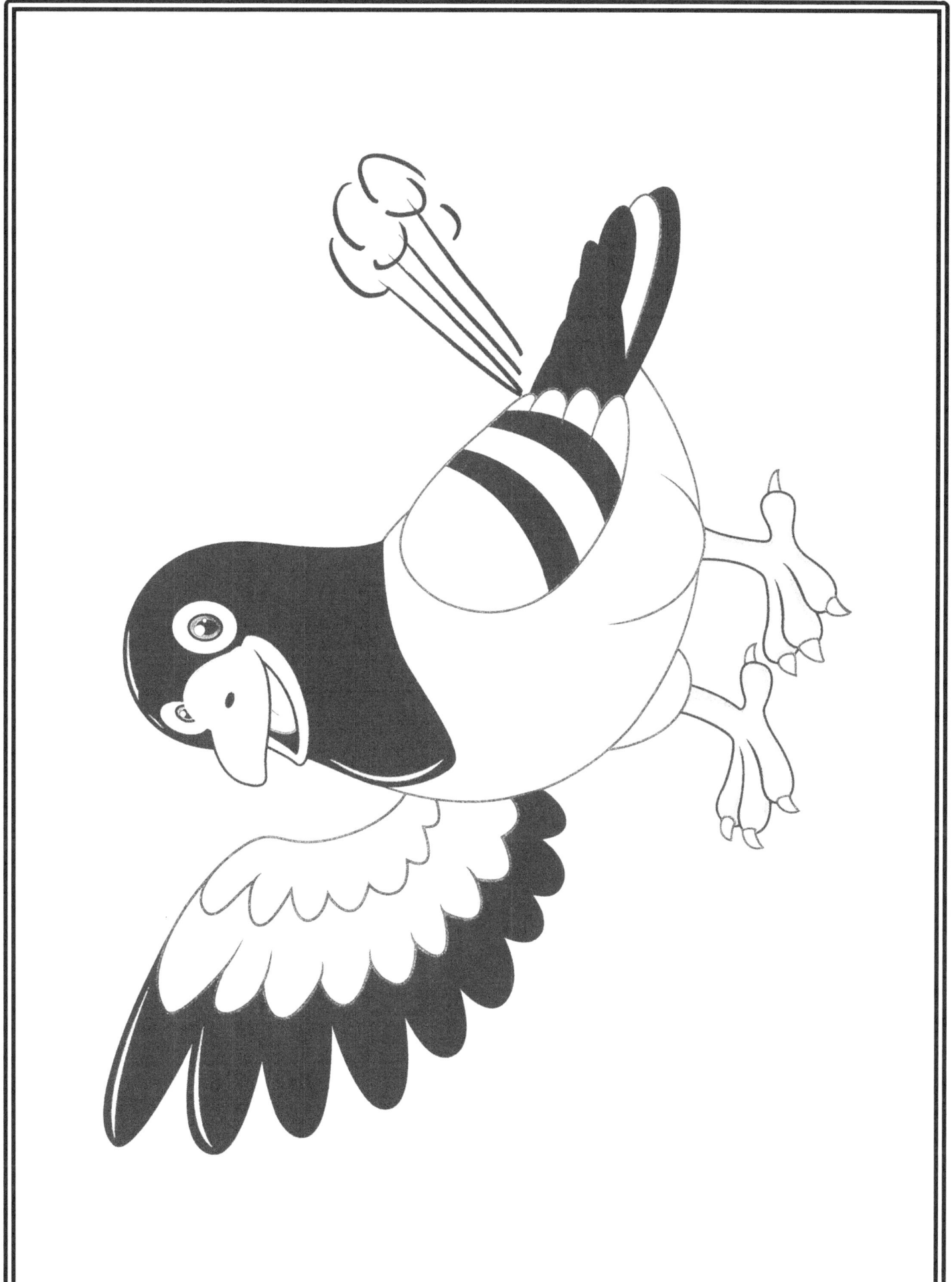

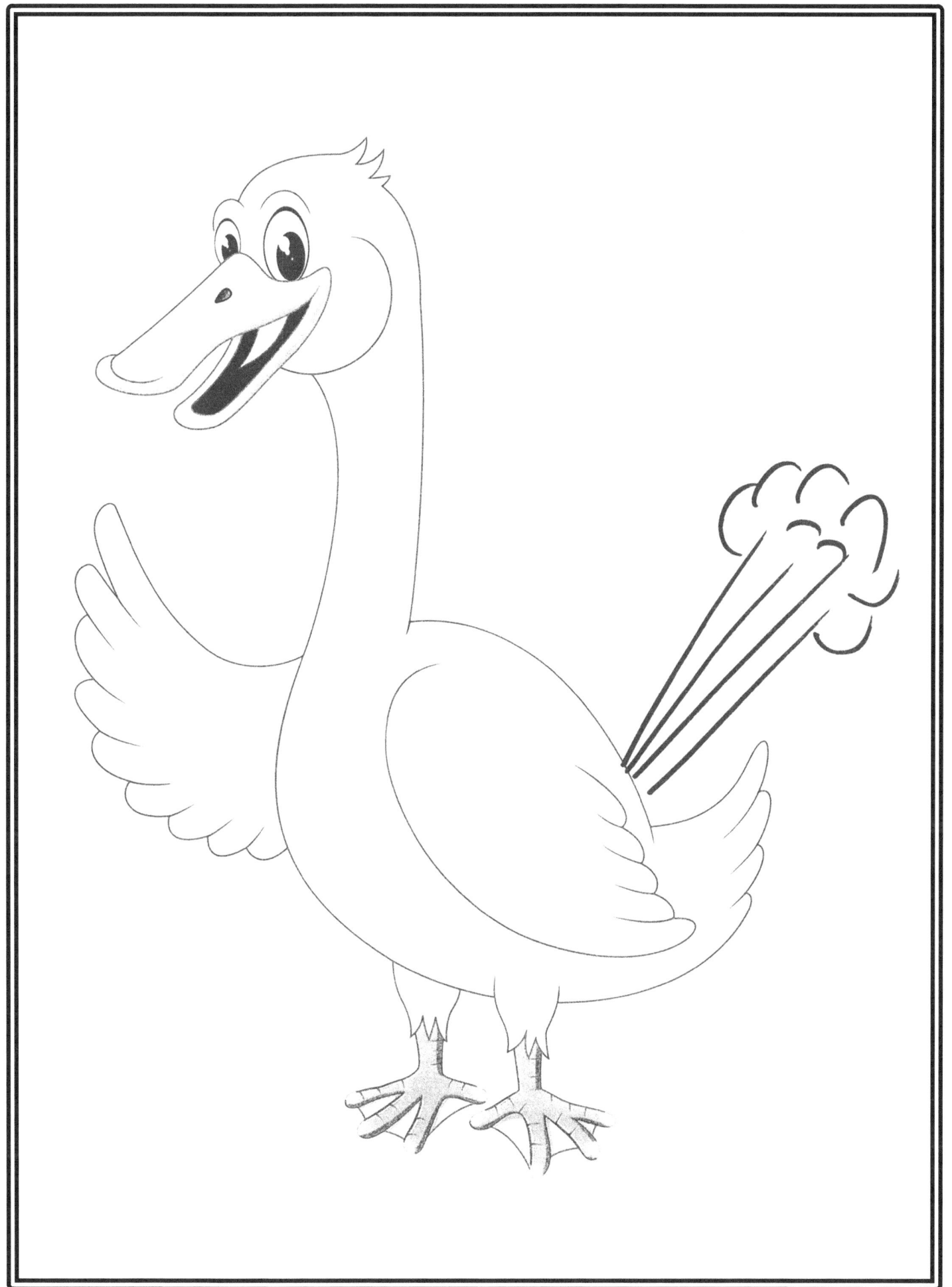

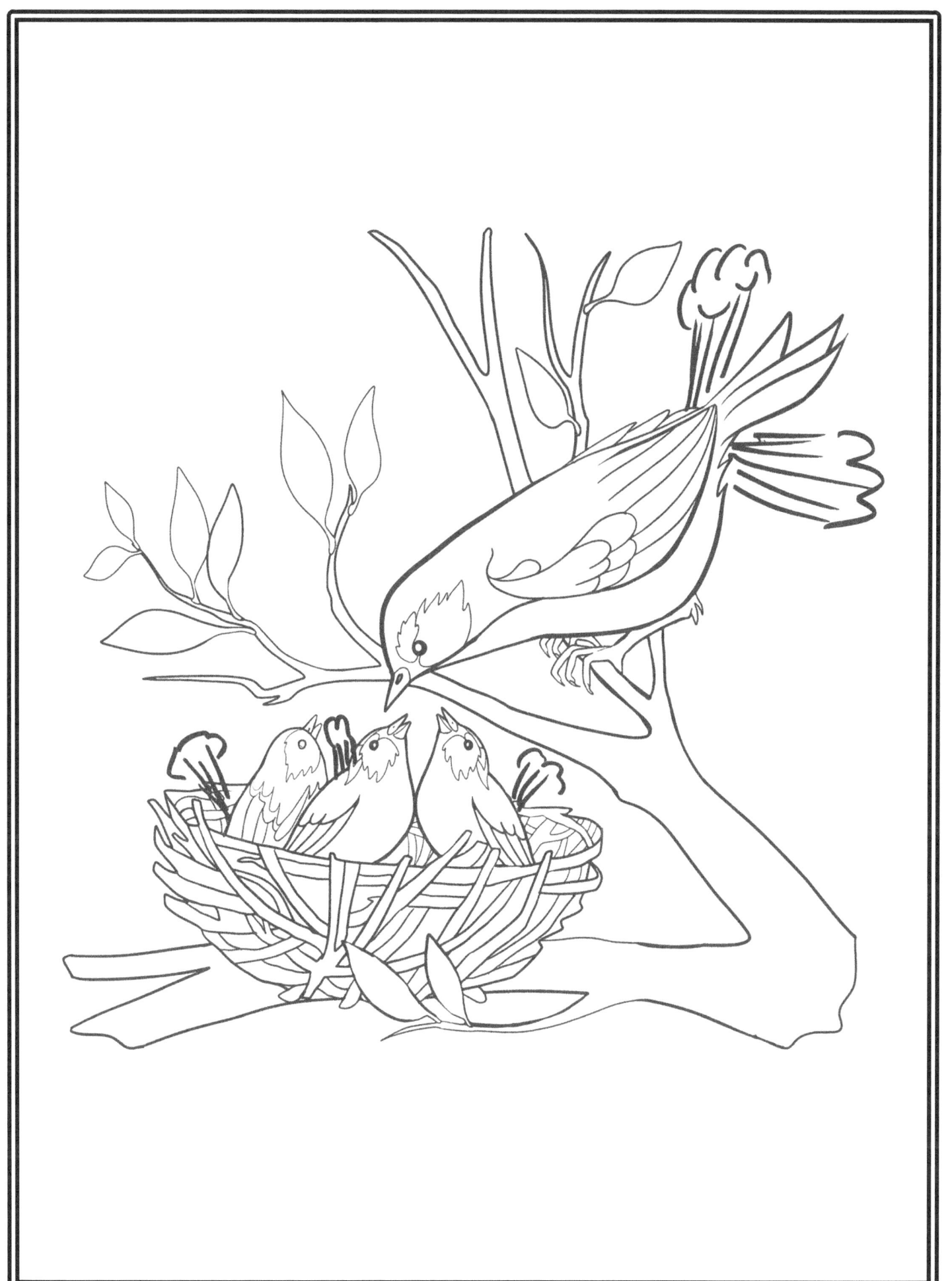

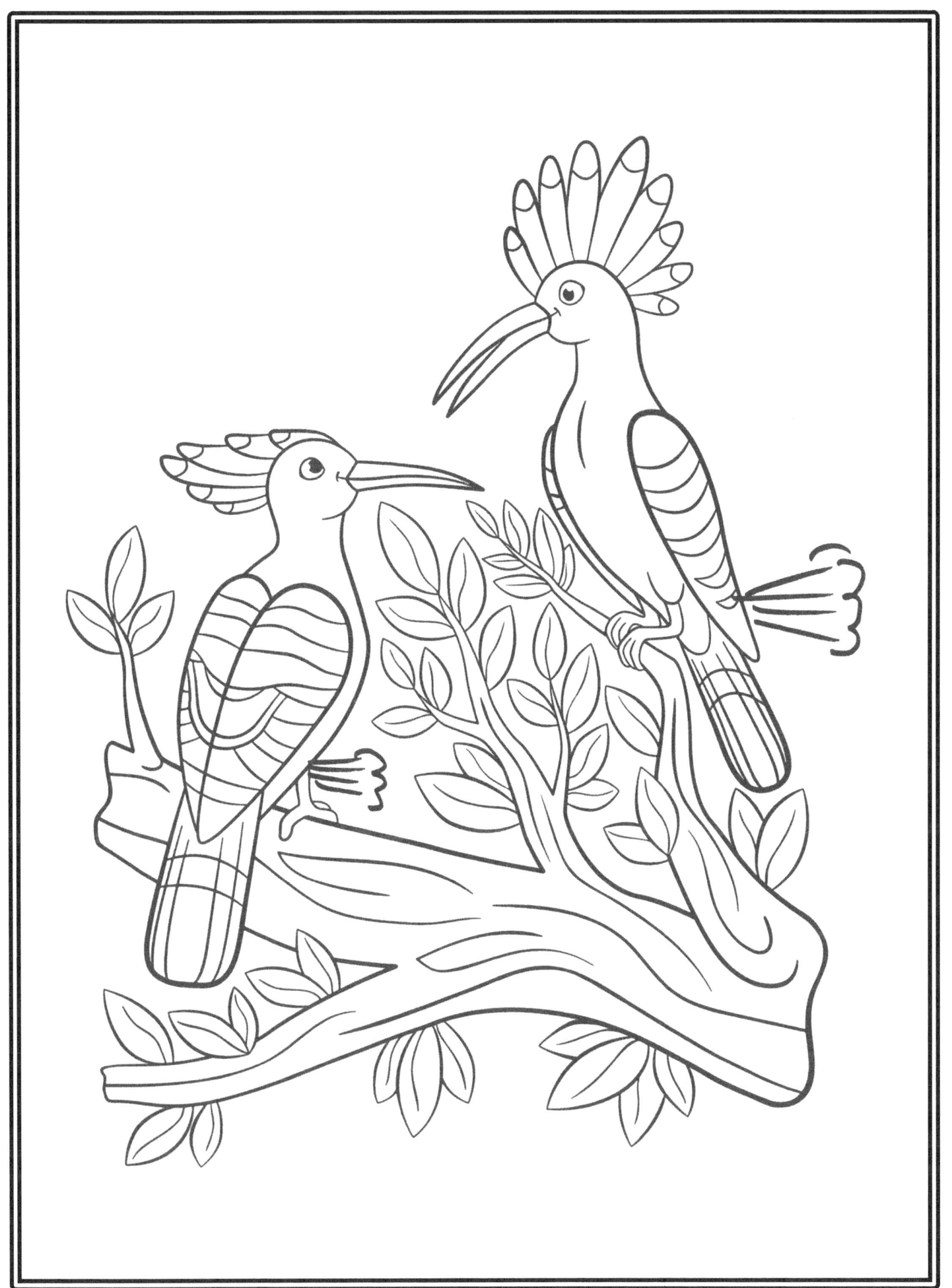

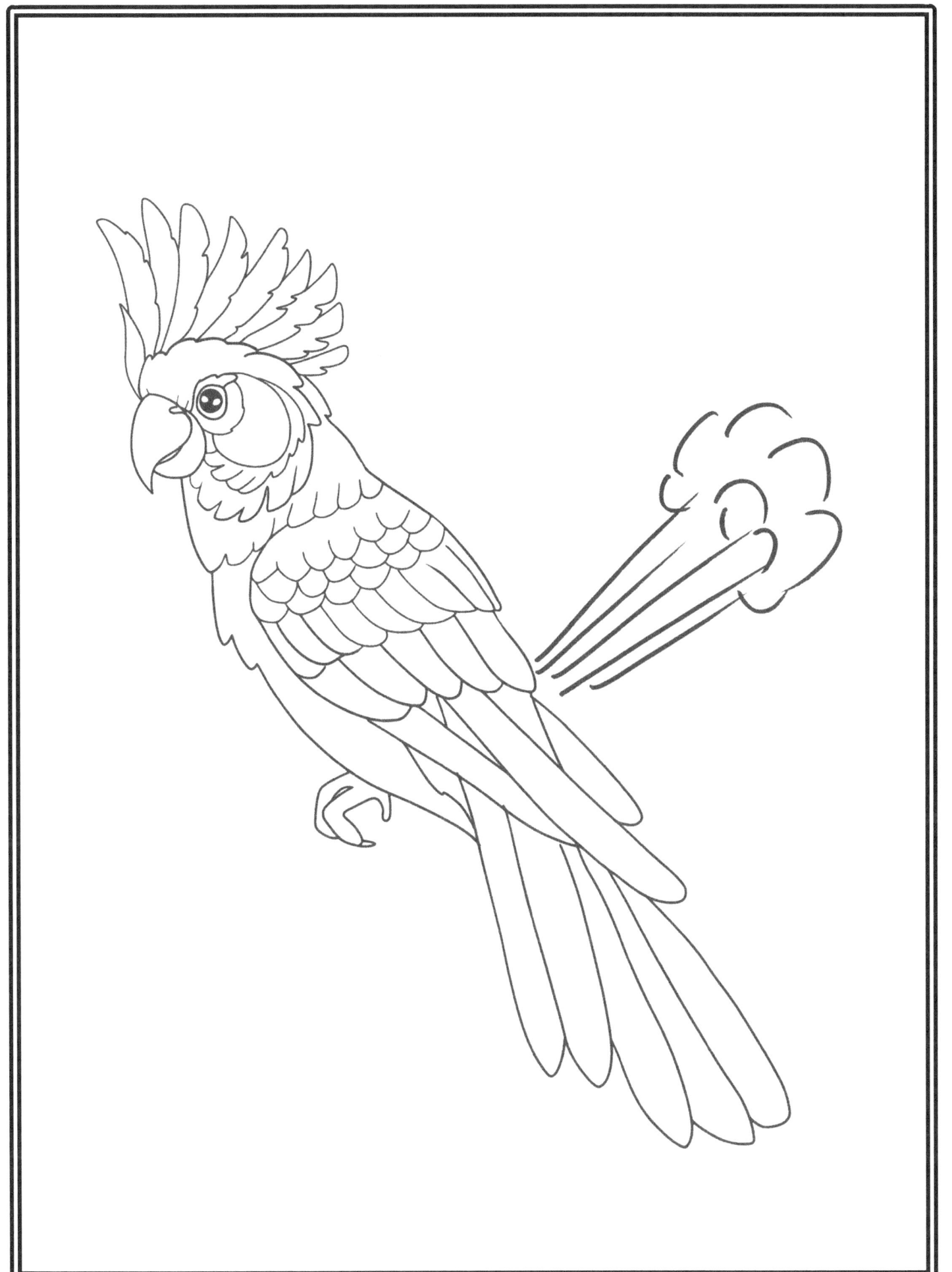

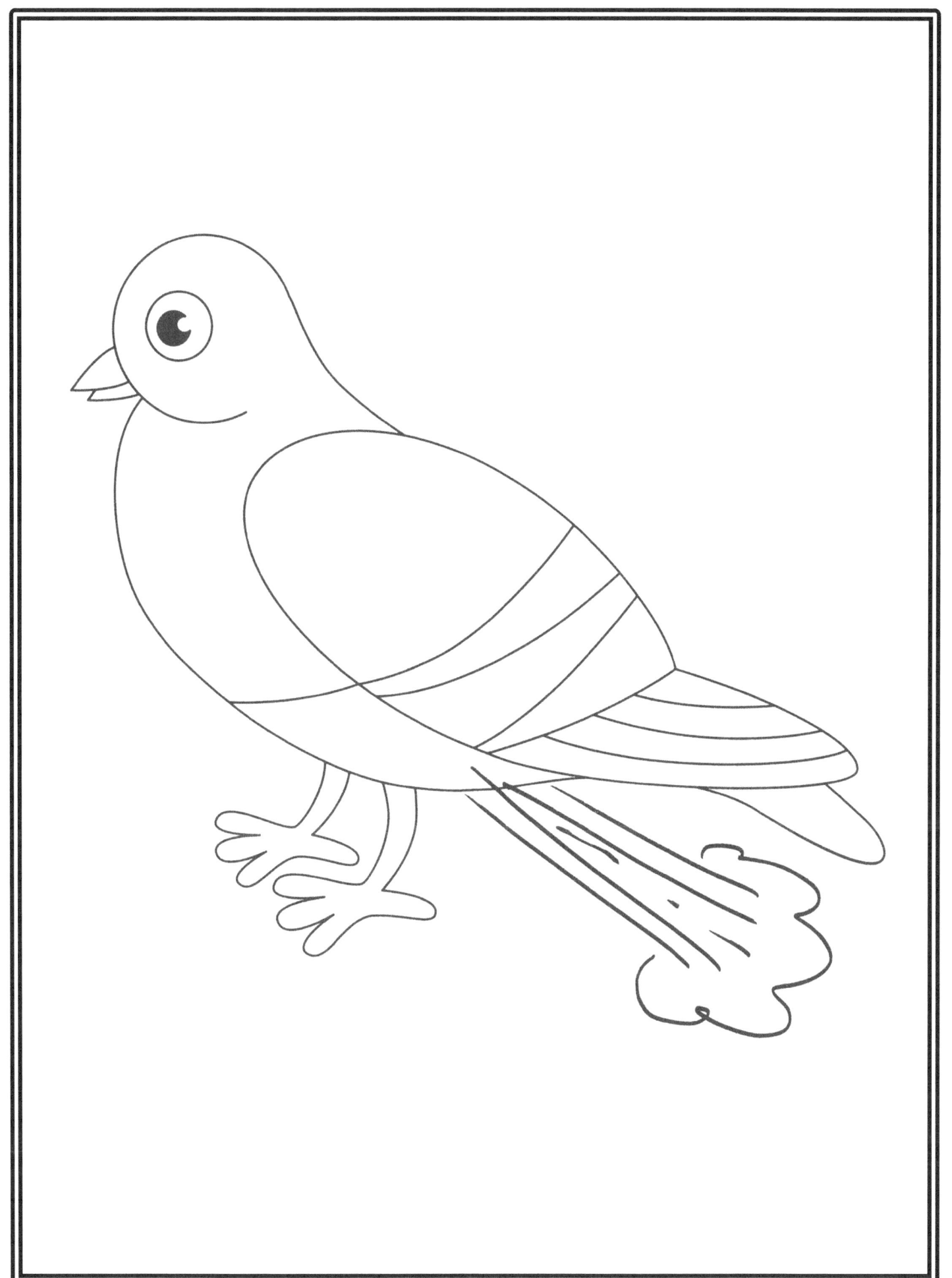

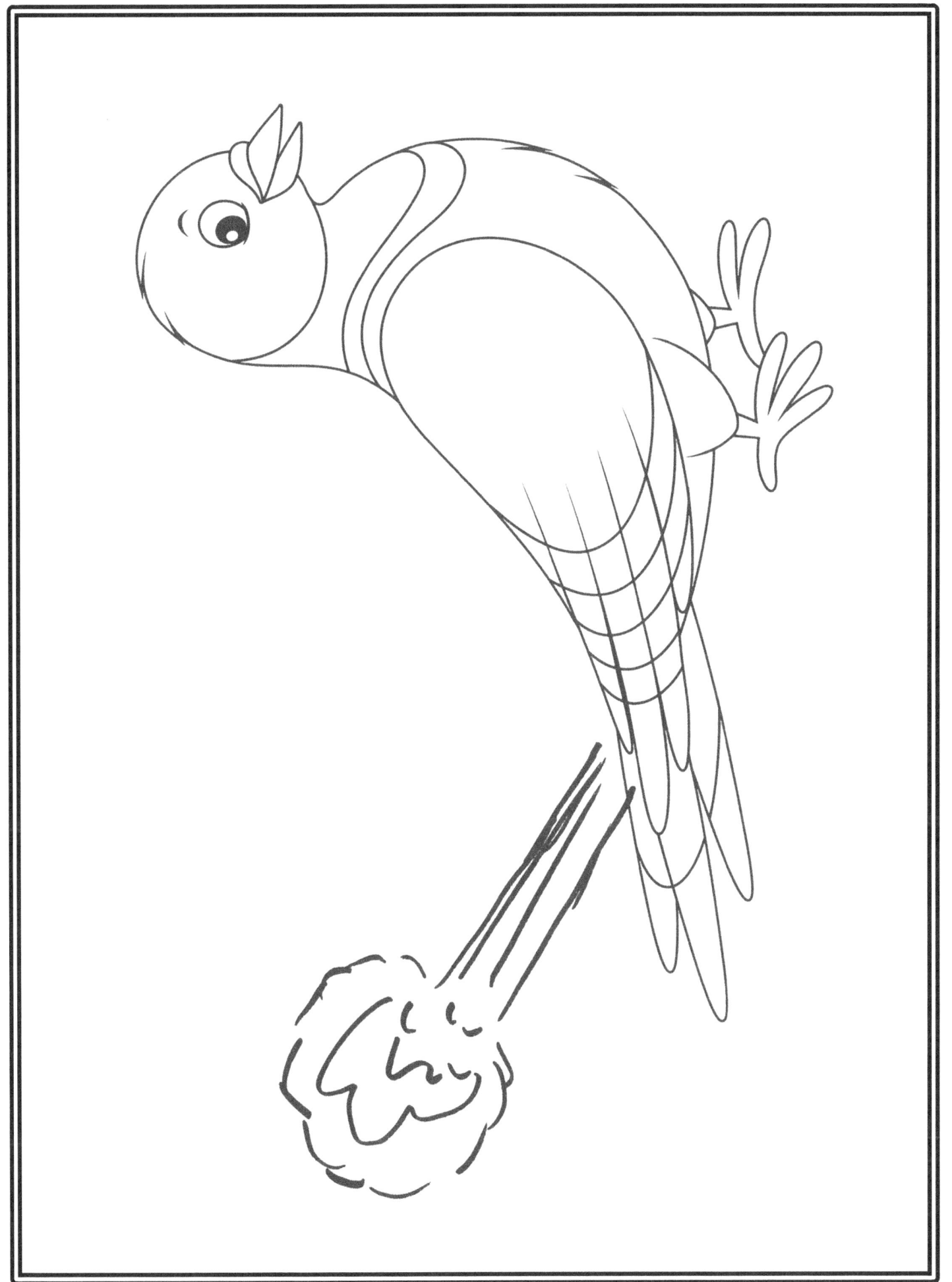

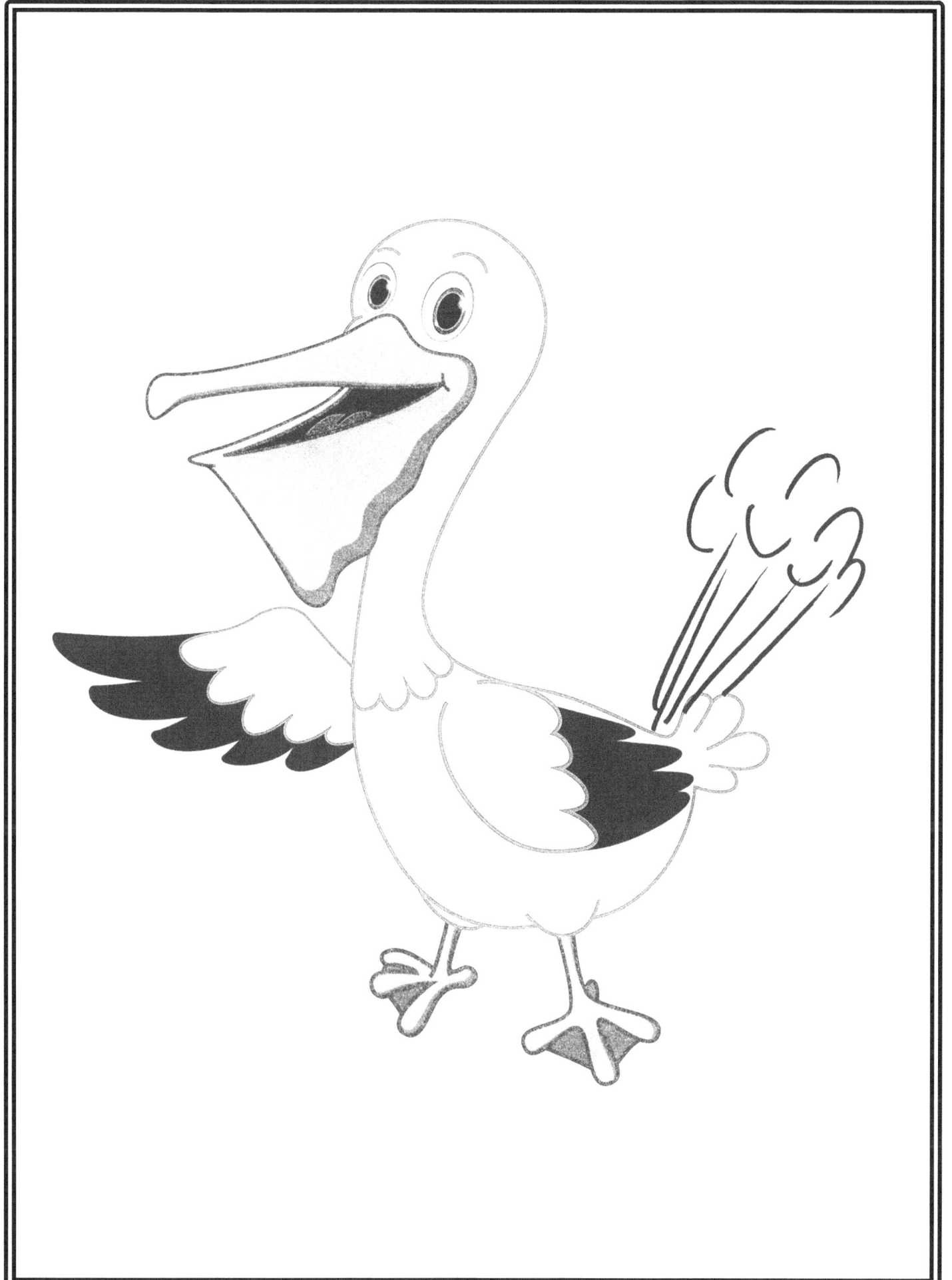

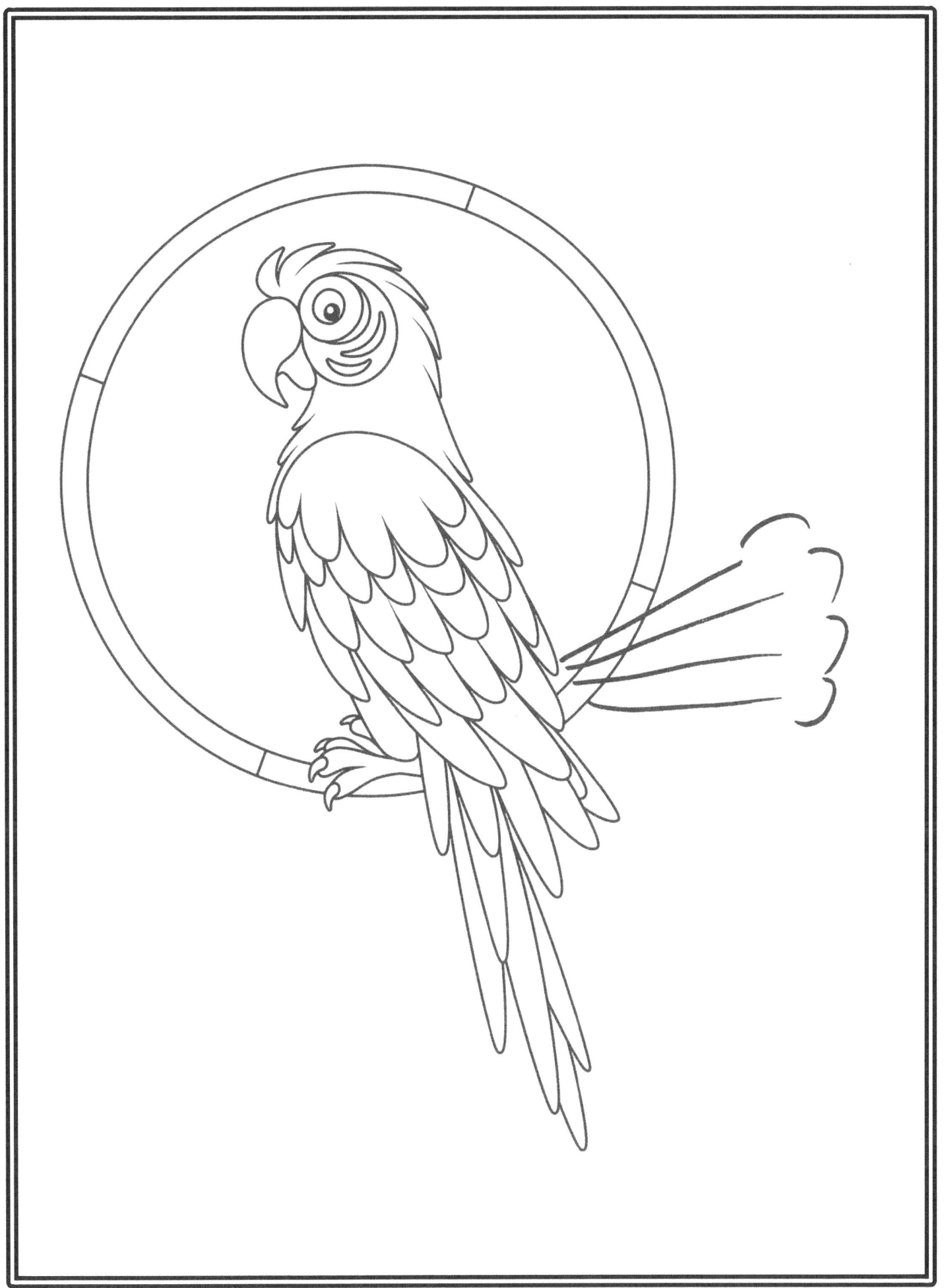

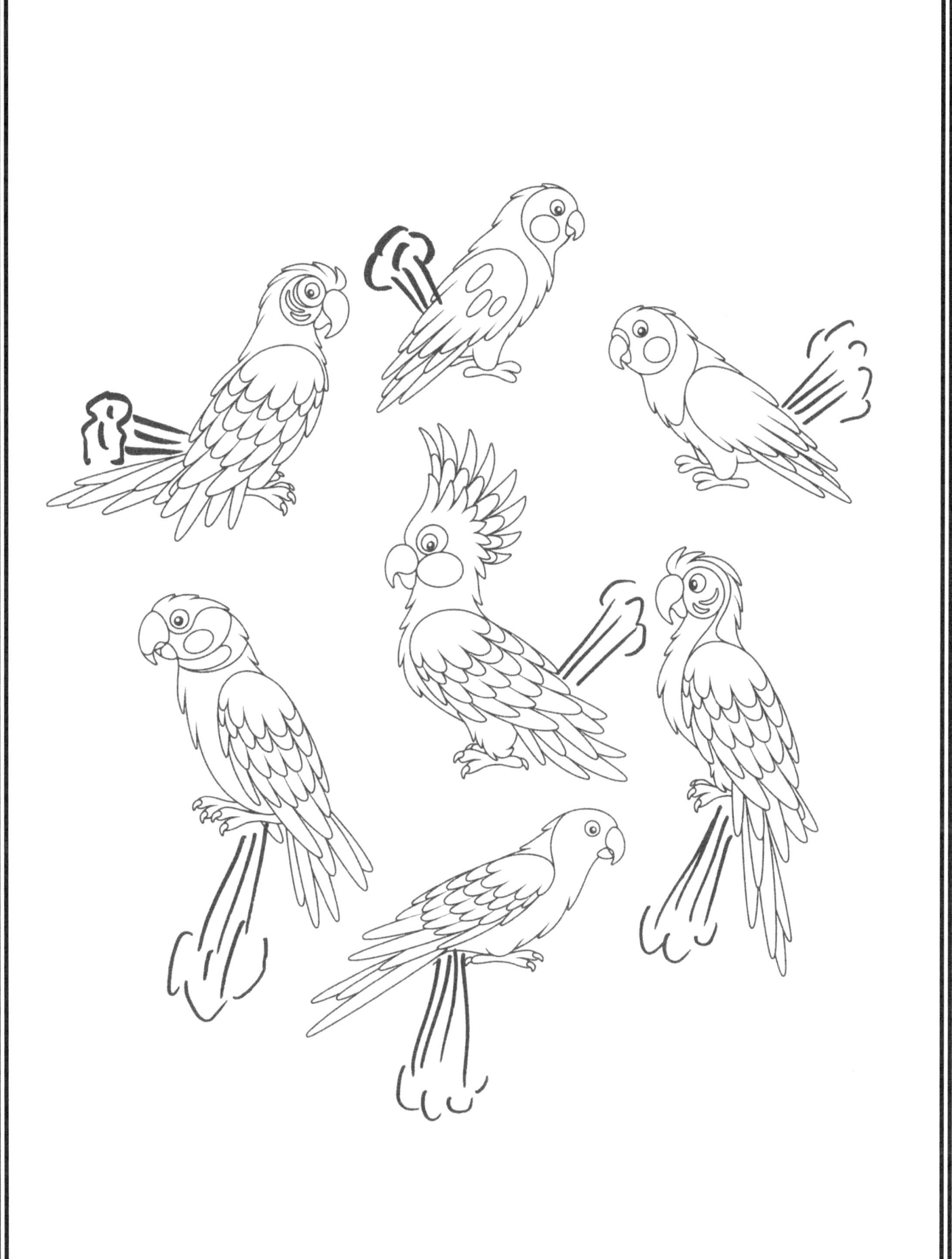

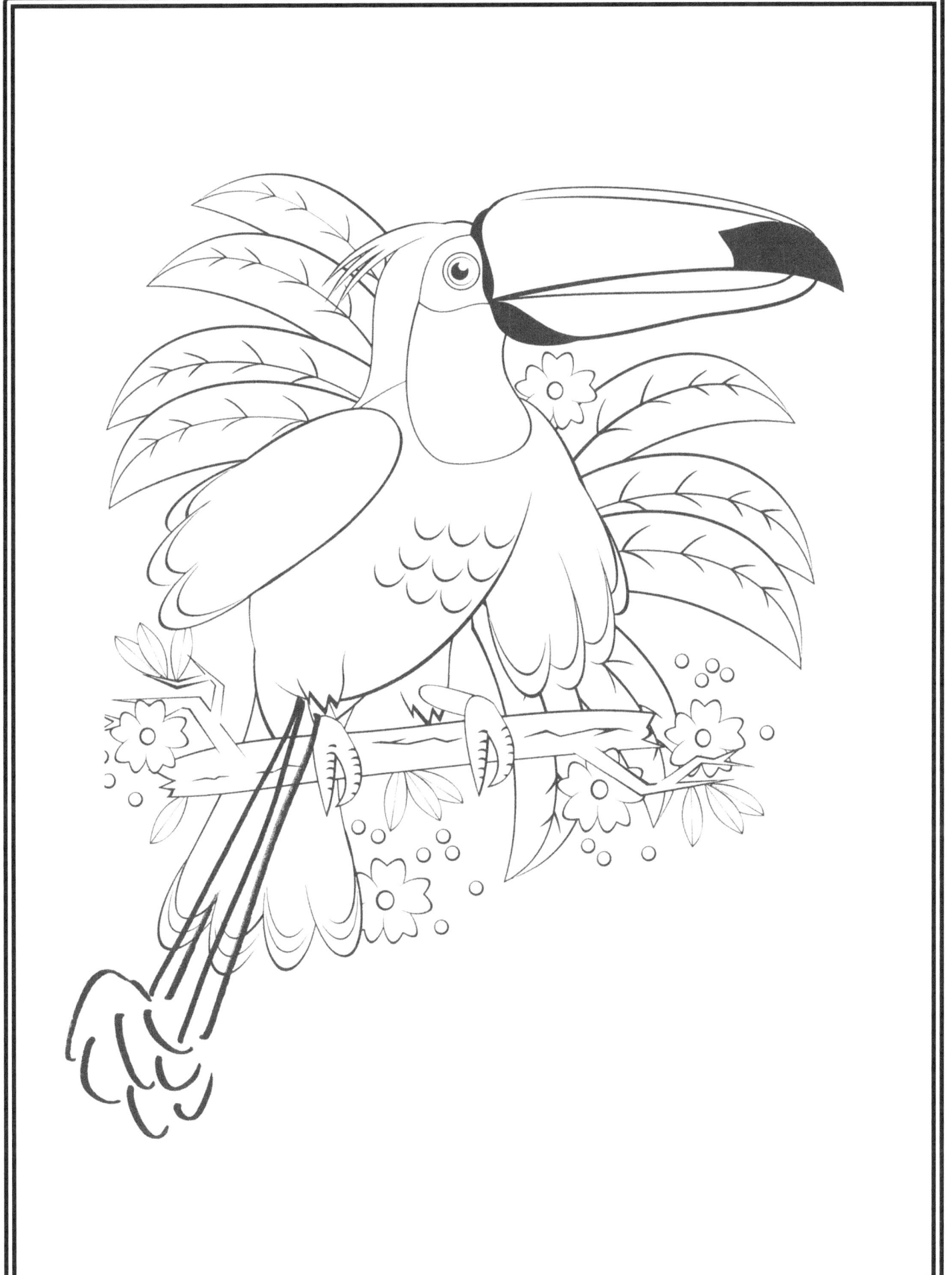

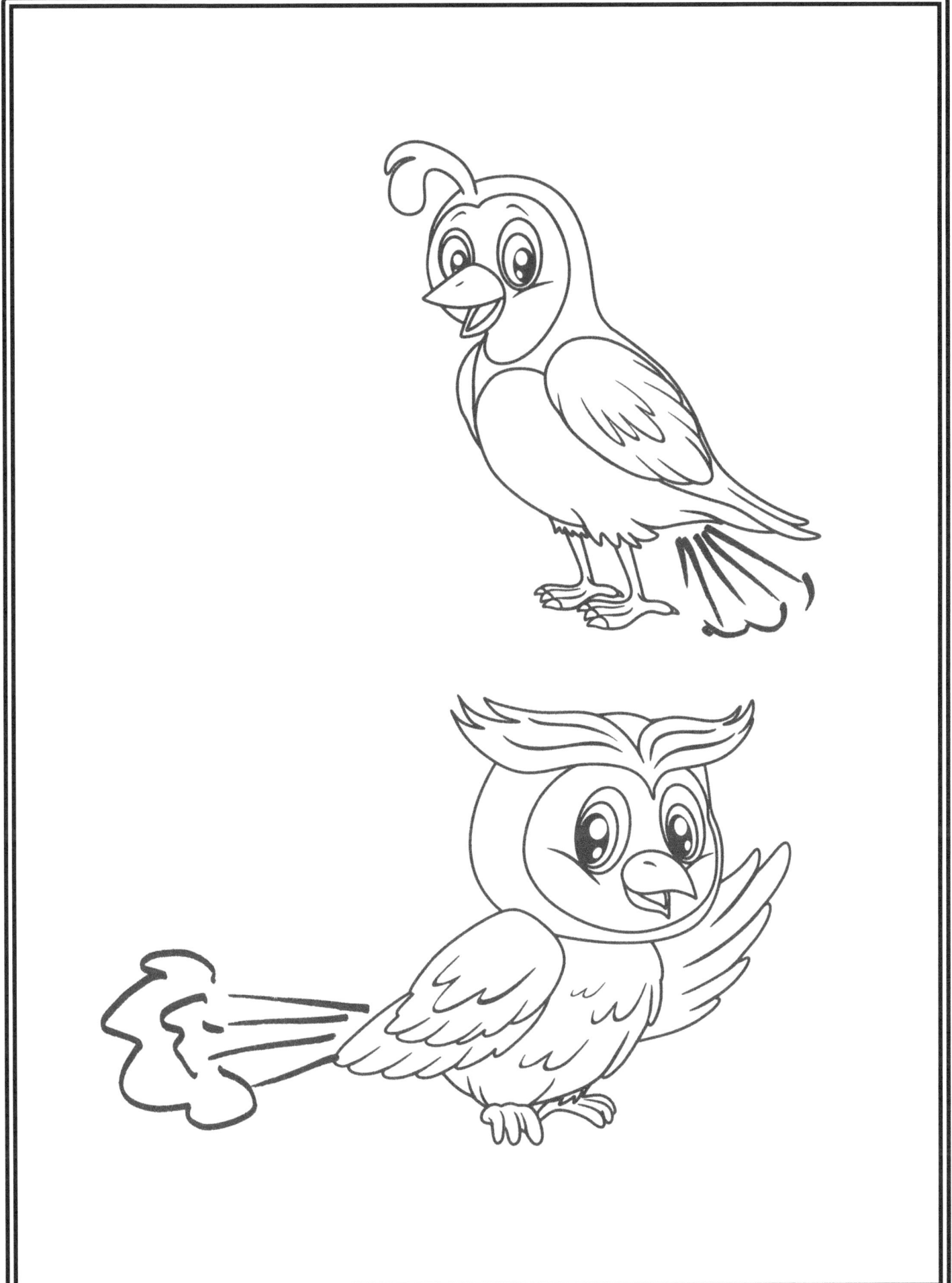

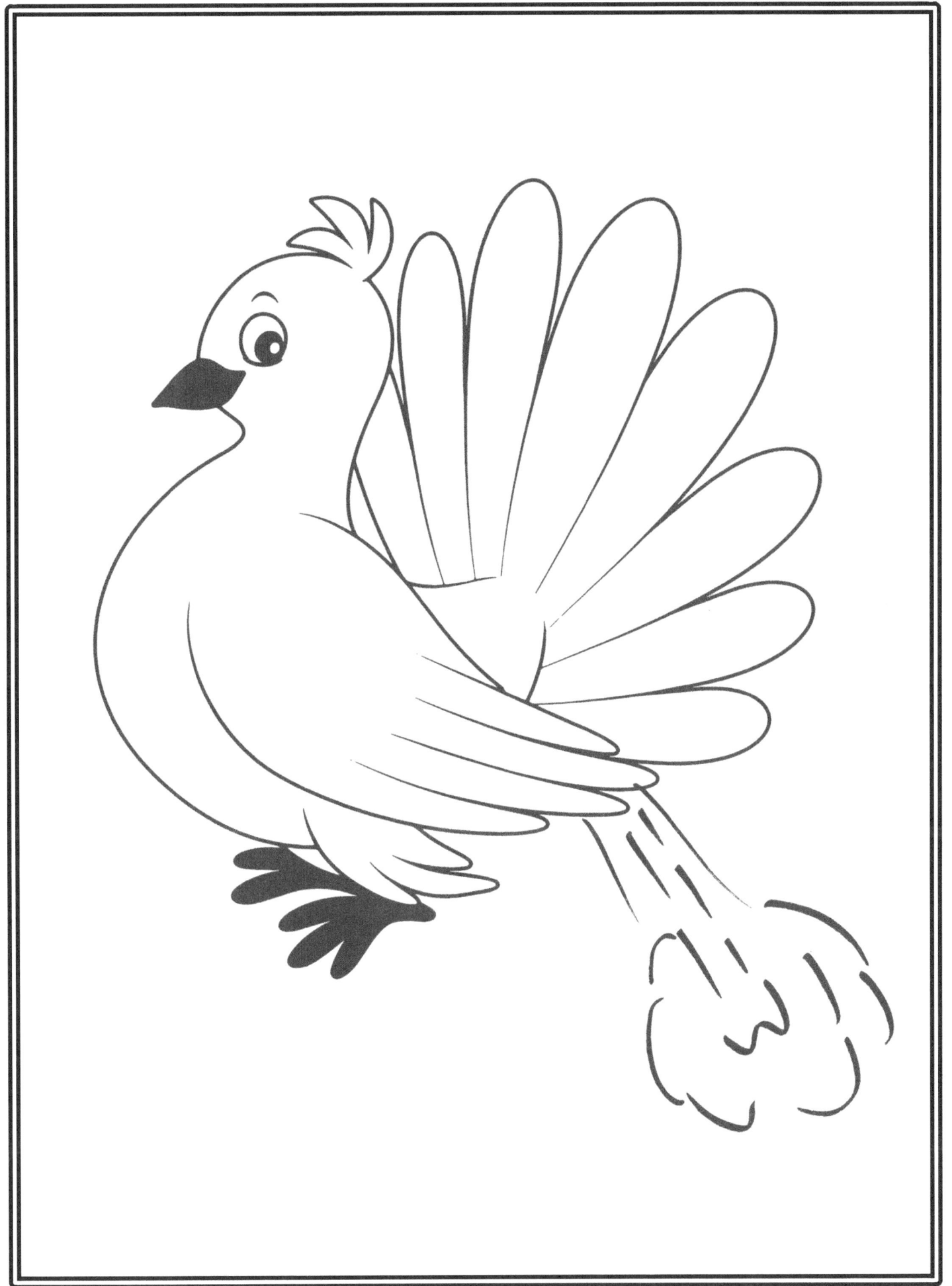

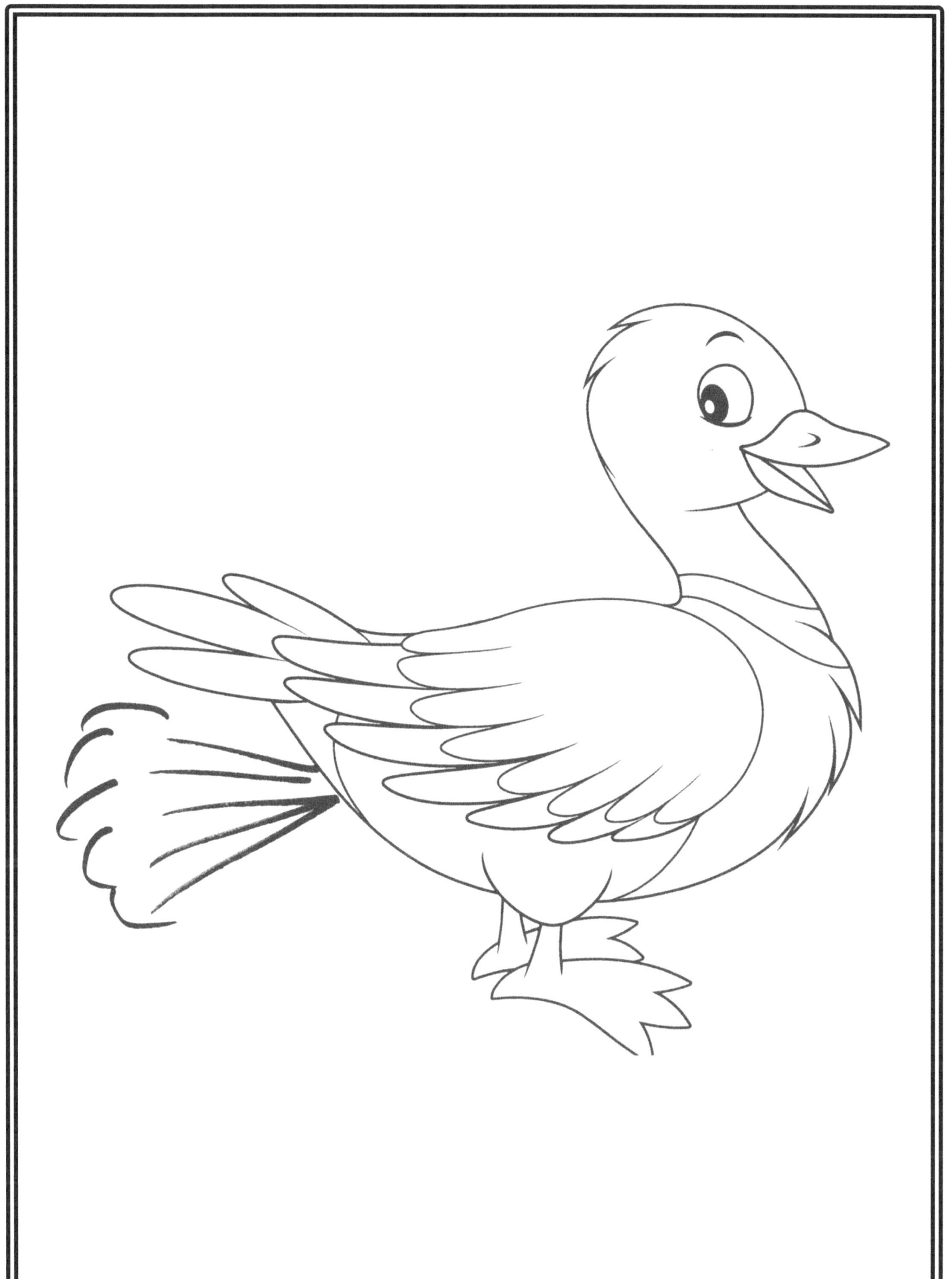

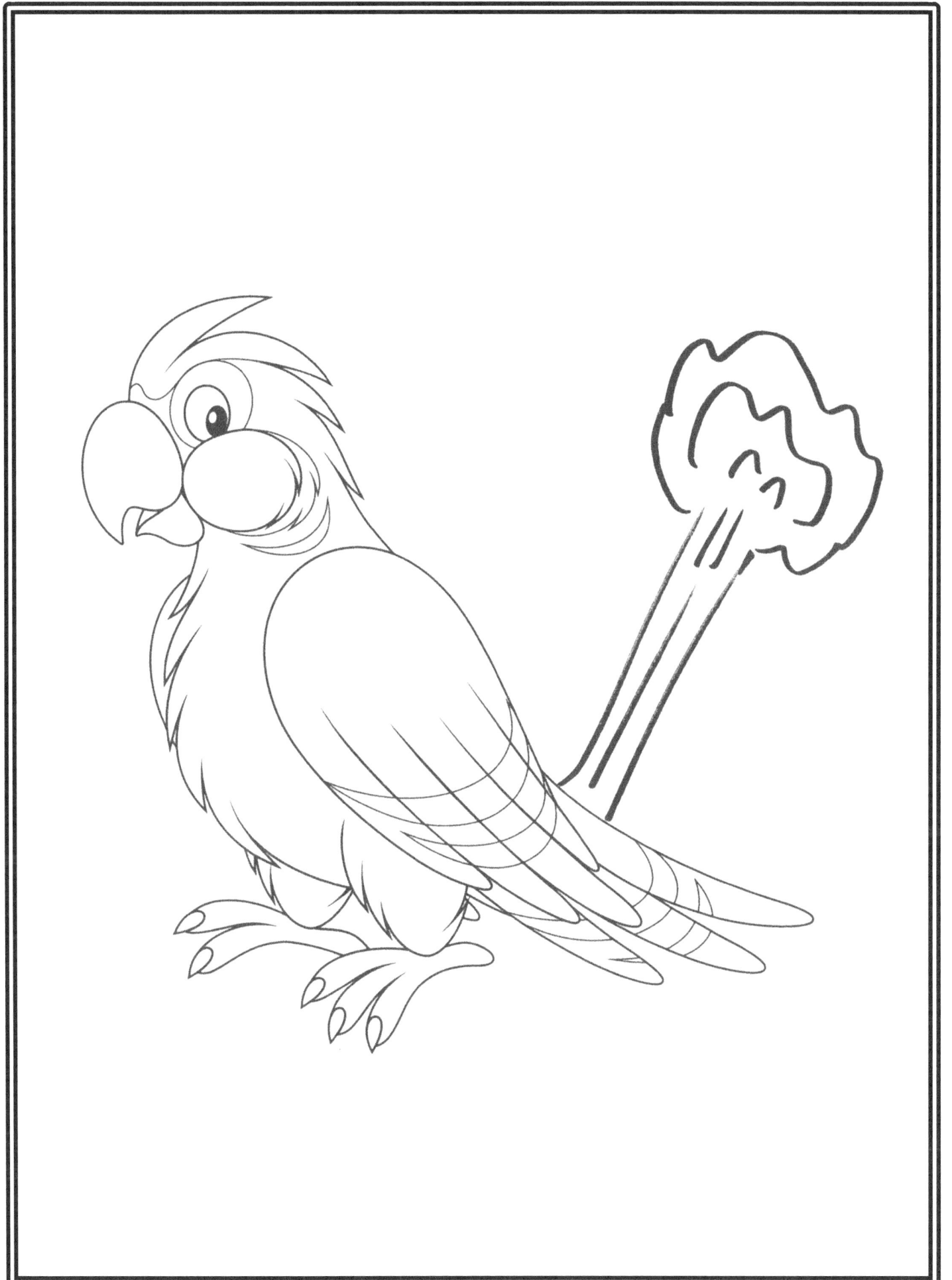

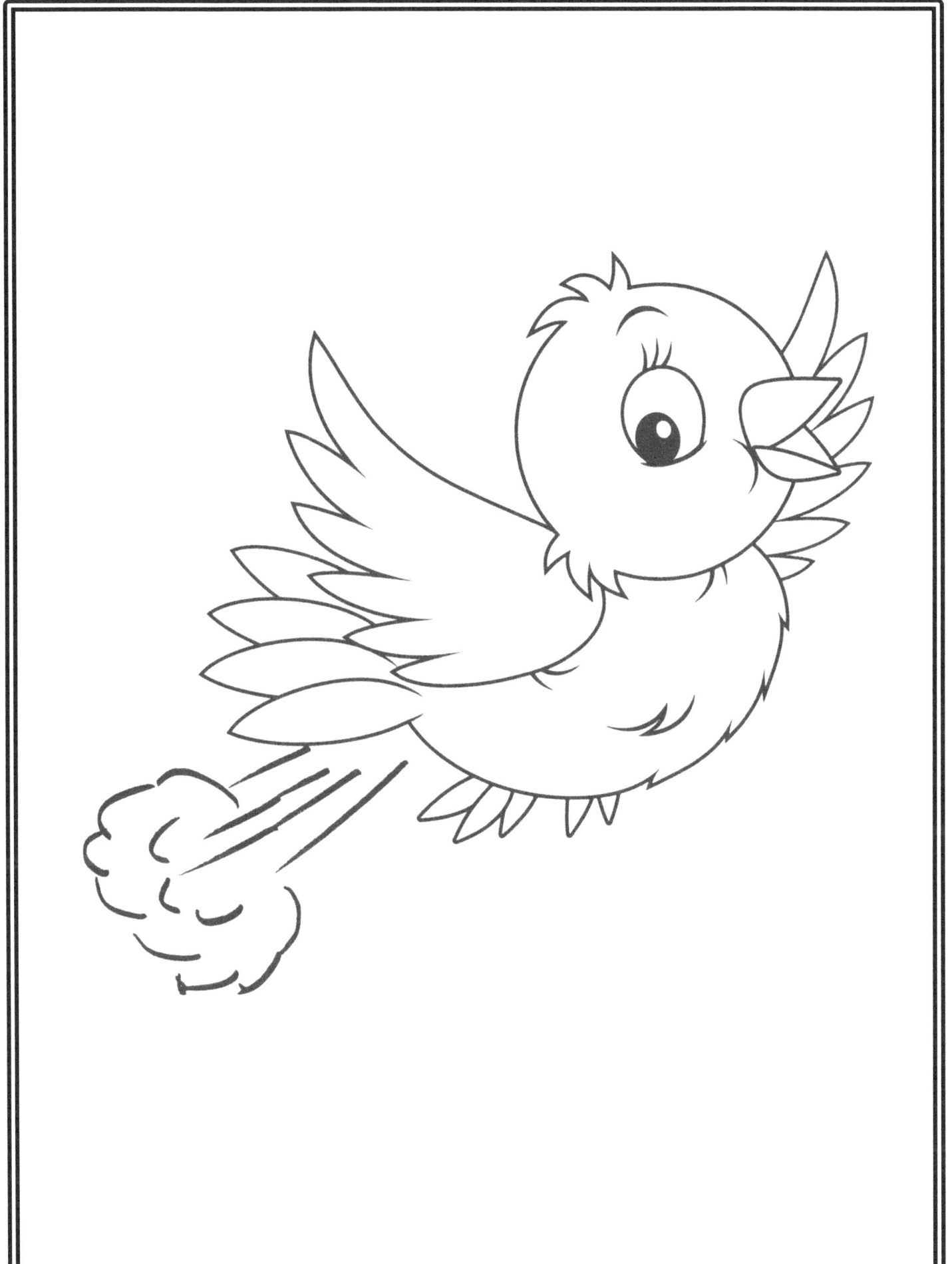

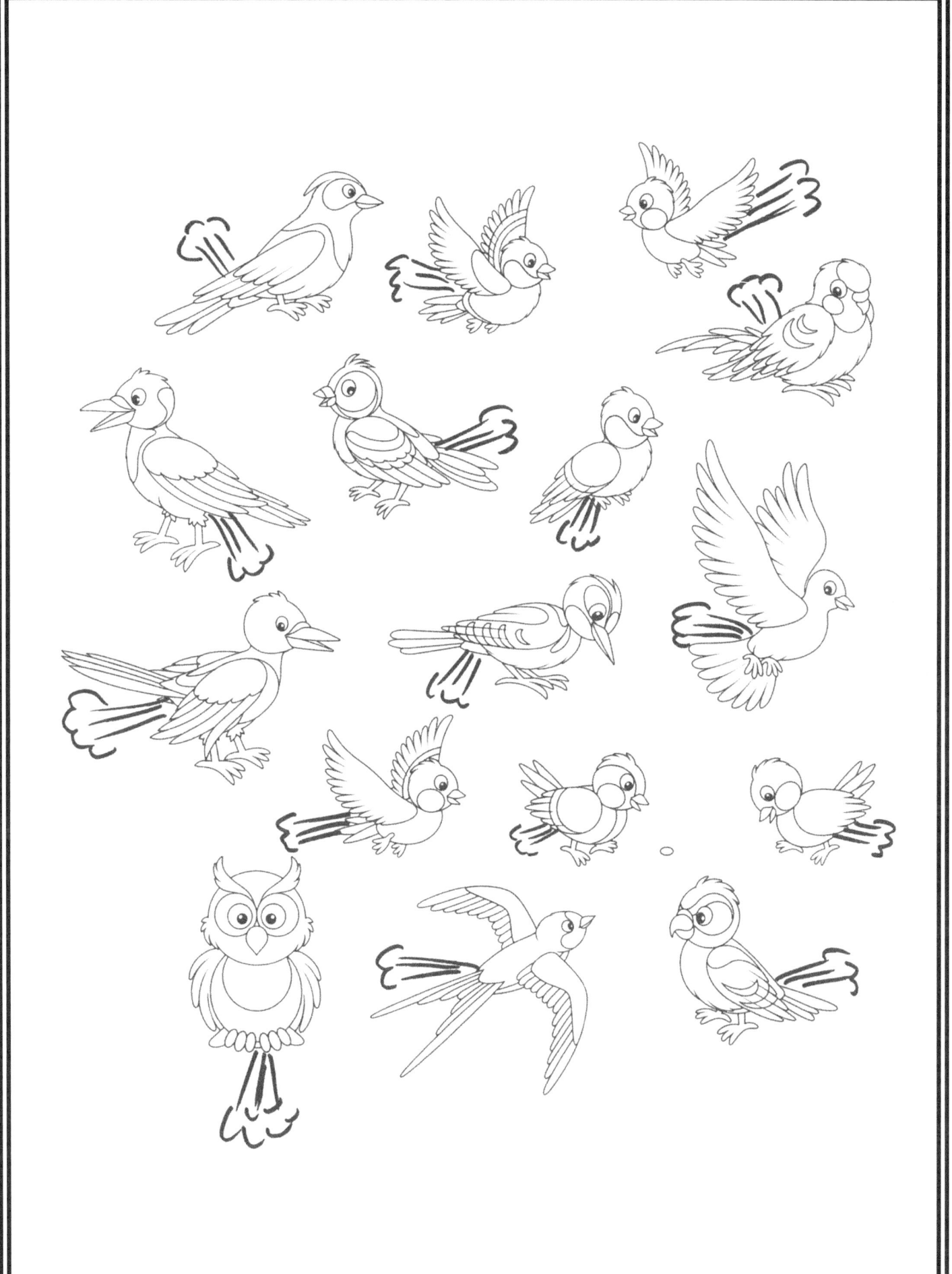

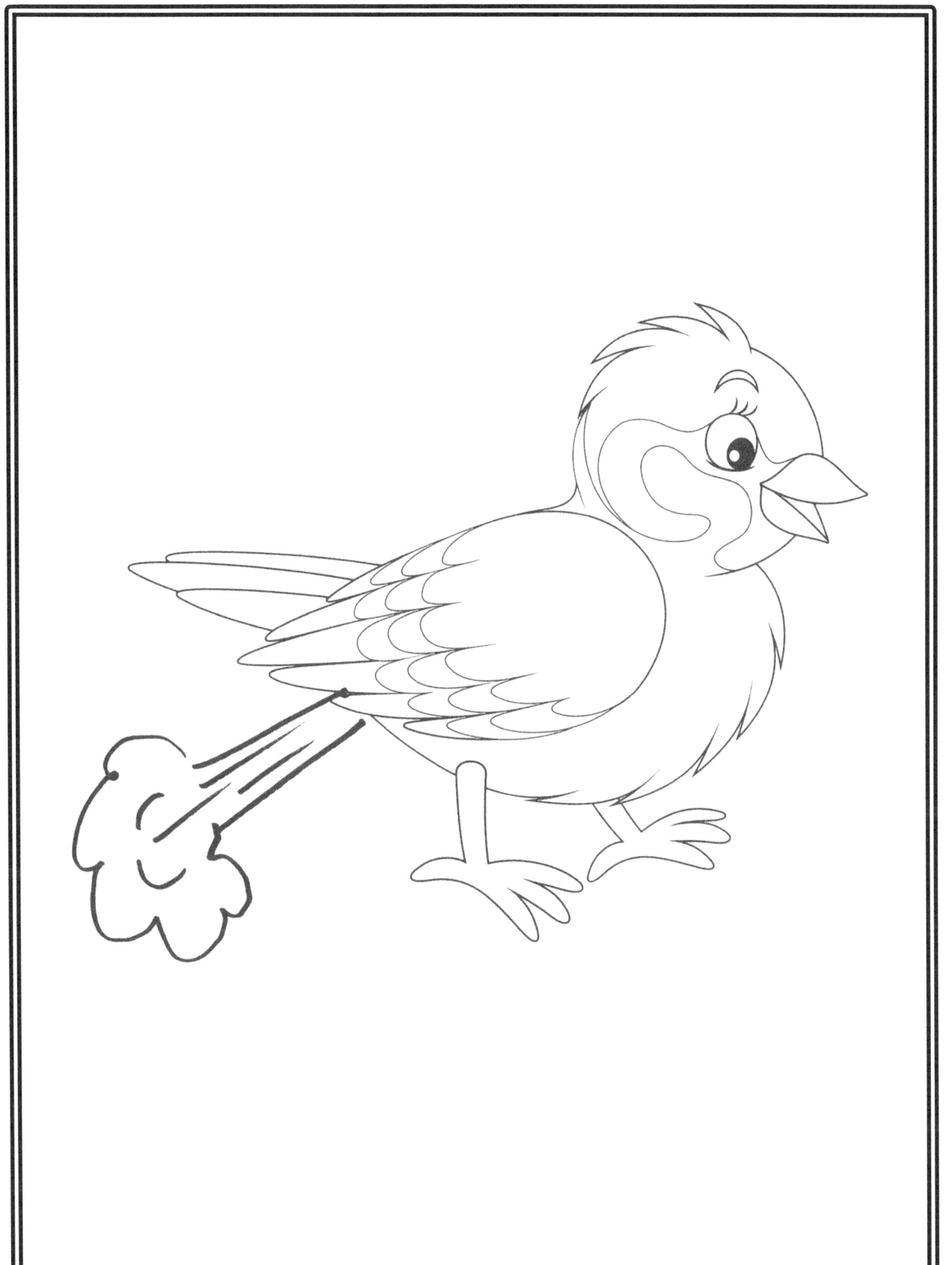